GODOT
GO DEO

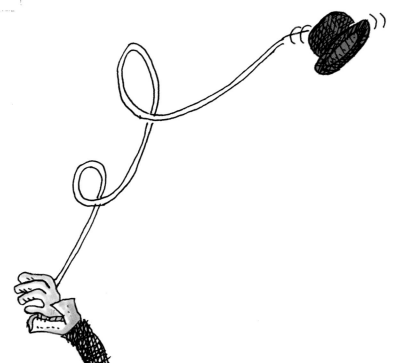

SAMUEL BECKETT made only a few specific references to Dublin in his work. However, in his short story "Fingal" in *More Pricks Than Kicks* he described the district, including the village of Feltrim, Lambay Island, the Naul and the 'brown woods' of Malahide Castle, as 'a land of sanctuary'. It seems appropriate therefore that Fingal Libraries should return the compliment with the publication of *Godot Go Deo* by the gifted artist Seán Lennon. I am therefore delighted to mark this special time in the Beckett calendar by inviting you to join young Sam and the Godot tramps on their nostalgic journey to the heart of Beckett's Dublin.

PAUL HARRIS, *Fingal County Librarian*

Godot Go Deo

Waiting in Beckett's Dublin

SEÁN LENNON

Foreword by
BARRY McGOVERN

FINGAL COUNTY COUNCIL

First published in 2006 by
FINGAL COUNTY LIBRARIES ✦ DUBLIN ✦ IRELAND
www.fingalcoco.ie

©Text and Illustrations Seán Lennon, 2006
Email: seanjlennon@gmail.com

ISBN: 0-9549103-1-1

This book is typeset by Ashfield Press in 11 on 16 point Obelisk
Colour Photography by JOHN HACKETT
Designed by SUSAN WAINE
Printed by BETAPRINT LTD, DUBLIN

Foreword by Barry McGovern

SAMUEL BECKETT HAD A GREAT SENSE OF HUMOUR. When a journalist once said to him 'You are English?' he replied 'Au contraire'. Despite living most of his life in France and his difficulties with his native land he always retained his Irish passport and had a strong loyalty to Ireland. He was, like Joyce, a Dubliner and, like Joyce, his writings are imbued with a sense of his native city.

In the early writings – *Dream of Fair to middling Women*, *More Pricks Than Kicks*, *Echo's Bones and Other Precipitates*, *Murphy* – Dublin locations are specific. From *Watt* onwards, and especially in the four novellas and the three great novels *Molloy*, *Malone Dies* and *The Unnamable*, the locations are not specified by name but are easily recognizable to any Dubliner.

Strangely, in one of his last prose works, *Company*, Dublin place names are specifically mentioned – Stepaside, Ballyogan Road, Croker's Acres, Connolly's Stores – the last two having been mentioned already in other works. There are also references to a neighbour, Mrs. Coote; to his father's car (a De Dion Bouton, mentioned in *The Old Tune*, his wonderful adaptation into rich Dublinese of Robert Pinget's *La manivelle*); and veiled references to his boyhood home Cooldrinagh and the 'Forty Foot' where he sometimes swam. So Dublin locations play a big role in Beckett's work.

Seán Lennon has not only provided an excellent introduction to the early life of Samuel Beckett but has given us hugely entertaining drawings and cartoons which capture the essence of Beckett's humour and unique vision. Beckett's only stage appearance was in a parody of Corneille's *Le Cid*. Beckett the writer was not averse to parody either. I'm sure he would have appreciated Seán Lennon's witty cartoons. Just as his last book *The Removal of Paddy Dignam* celebrated the centenary of Bloomsday, this book celebrates what has been described as the Gloomsday centenary.

In *Endgame* Hamm says at one point: 'Don't we laugh?' The fact that Clov replies 'I don't feel like it' doesn't mean we can't. Like O'Casey whom he admired, Beckett mixed the tragic and the comic in equal measure. This admixture is one of the features of Irish humour. As Molloy says: 'Tears and laughter, they are so much Gaelic to me'. And remember *Waiting for Godot* is, in Beckett's own words, a tragicomedy. There are so many far-too-serious and gloomy articles and tomes written about Beckett that it's a relief to welcome a book that is light and humorous. *Godot Go Deo* gets right to the spirit of Sam Beckett - a man who, though too sensitive to fit easily into the world, leavened its horrors with fierce humour.

MARCH 2006

Authors Note

IMAGINE WE HAVE A NEW AND HAPPY SAMUEL BECKETT on our hands. One who on receiving the news of his Nobel Prize for literature decided that life's pendulum was on the upswing. He determined, despite humanity's noticeable dip in form of late, that if he had truly 'arrived' then writing a neurotic romantic comedy could be the way to go. Suppose that he decided he'd suffered enough for his art, went forth and 'got a life' embracing celebrity as the thinking woman's alpha-male existentialist crumpet. In short, imagine that when the turning point in coverage of Beckett came, he sold out. We all know Samuel Beckett wouldn't or indeed couldn't reduce himself to a human pit-stop for the literary tourist. In fact, on becoming more celebrated than any other living writer, Beckett did the opposite of what was expected, making himself conspicuous by his absence and rarer than a visitation from the redoubtable Mr. Godot.

What's scarce is of course wonderful and so we wondered what it was exactly we'd been missing prior to 1969. Instantly, his picture was everywhere. Although of Huguenot descent at first glance he seemed a dead ringer for the *sean-nós* singer and storyteller Seósamh O hÉanaí, who had a face like chiselled granite. On closer inspection, however, it was obvious Beckett had an air of intellectual incision you could cut butter with, and the sharpest, most aquiline features ever spotted outside of an aviary.

It became 'trendy' to read *Murphy*. Everybody at 'The Blind' had the bell bottom pants but if you hadn't done the required reading, word was, you could forget it. I was a teenager but more than ready for the difficult and dark stories of Mr Beckett, having already explored the romantic, semi-Gothic world of the Irish ghost-story writer, Joseph Sheridan Le Fanu. I knew *Murphy* was a brilliantly funny cult book. What I didn't know was that as a chat-up line it would tend to go down like a luke-warm mineral. In order to advance I retreated back to discuss the current 'track', tight-lipped but insistent that Samuel Beckett's *Murphy* was far less depressing than *Honey* by Bobby Goldsboro.

In the 70s RTE showed the BBC 2 production of *Krapp's Last Tape* featuring the Armagh actor Patrick Magee, who had played Alfredo to Vincent Price's Prospero in *The Masque of the Red Death* and a good number of journeyman roles in low budget horror films to which he always brought a touch of class. However, the stage was his medium and films were seen as a way of financing his real career. He became synonymous with Beckett. His Krapp still remains the definitive version. I haven't watched it for some thirty odd (one or two very odd) years but can still see Magee: glowering, malignant, addled. He played it like it was written for him, which of course it had been. 'The only play I ever wrote with an actor in mind' said Beckett 'was *Krapp's Last Tape*, which I dedicated to Patrick Magee'.

Beckett: 'What's up, Krapp?'
Krapp: 'I'm out of tapes.'

The middle to late Beckett was the artistic off-spring of the Second World War. If man had ever been the measure of all things, the twentieth century put paid to that. In this light, dismissing Beckett as 'too grim' is about as useful as reporting that one's local TD is 'good as gold'. However, certain names and places stimulate fixed responses. On mentioning Edgar Allan Poe's "The Premature Burial" your first free-association might be 'the day job'. Mention *Waiting for Godot* and my first free-association – well, second perhaps after 'waiting for the Dart' – is of the sheer joy of that play as performed by Barry McGovern, Johnny Murphy, Stephen Brennan and Alan Stanford.

On foot of a real-life scam in which he was intended as the unwitting victim, Beckett wrote 'The difference between being done and being done in the eye is that in the first case one

knows and in the second not. He thinks he is doing me in the eye, whereas he is only doing me. That is the diverting position that I would not spoil with the least show of discernment'. Perhaps we'd be better off taking umbrage at the presumption of Clov in *Endgame* when, having given us a good telescopic once-over, he comments: 'I see...a multitude...in transports...of joy. (Pause). That's what I call a magnifier'. Is Clov doing us in the eye? Could Beckett be having us all on? Is the Pope a Catholic? Do bed bugs bite?

Hamm's wonderfully grandiose question to himself in *Endgame*: 'Can there be misery loftier than mine?' is a masterpiece of unbridled self-importance verging on religiosity. Hamm is hard to take without squirming and, let's face it, no matter what his circumstances are, they couldn't possibly be as dreadful as ours! The monstrous Hamm was served with perfect self-relish by Drimnagh's finest, Michael Gambon, at the Albery Theatre, London, in 2004. Lee Evans played Clov in the same production. All may be 'corpsed' but Clov discovers he still has to contend with living fleas.

In reviewing *Murphy* Dylan Thomas described Samuel Beckett as 'a great leg-puller'. Do we, you may ask, really need another leg-puller in the one-legged race of life? Perhaps not, but comedy is what Beckett is about. If an ability to listen to Mozart's *Piano Concerto No. 21* without thinking of your one *Elvira Madigan* can be seen as a sign of intellectual discernment, could viewing the various Beckett pairs without thinking of Laurel and Hardy, be another?

Godot's deafening silences between dialogues are pure Laurel and Hardy. Silent mimes introduce both *Endgame* and *Krapp's Last Tape*. Like the Acme Silence Man Beckett's aim was to make silences 'more competent-ly than ever a better man spangled the butterflies of vertigo'. The presence of mime and prevalence of silence throughout the work suggest Beckett still had a hankering after early sound and silent film. In fact his only known public appearance on stage was at the Peacock Theatre in 1931 in *Le Kid*. This revue, which he co-wrote, had strong echoes of Charlie Chaplin's *The Kid*. Beckett played The Kid's father with a flowing white beard and bowler hat.

Beckett's media work was to bring him into contact with a visionary icon of American cinema, Buster Keaton. As Beckett put it, Keaton's face was his 'trump card'. Known in his later career to bring his first-rate talents to second-rate projects, this was the first time Keaton had worked on anything quite as radical as *FILM*, which was shot on location in a stiflingly hot New York in 1964. Although he was quick to vol-

unteer the information that he didn't know 'what the hell was going on' Keaton never complained from day one. I would love to have seen Buster and Sam together. What should have been a dream team didn't quite work out that way. Beckett, in Buster's view, was 'nuts' but Buster gave his all. Keaton, according to Beckett, was 'inaccessible. He had a poker mind as well as a poker face'.

'One of the first things we did' said Beckett 'was to find the location – driving all over New York, looking for the wall – which we eventually found at the (Fulton Street) Fish Market – near Brooklyn Bridge...when I saw that face at the end – oh!'

Meeting James Joyce, for whom he became a trusted personal assistant, marked a pivotal moment in Beckett's life. Joyce rubbed off on Beckett the novelist, before Beckett the embroiled dramatist introduced himself. Dublin was a way to the heart 'of all the cities of the world' for Joyce, while Beckett saw the world as perilous and man as irrational. And so after Joyce's maximalism came Beckett's minimalism and where, in time of doubt, Joyce left it in, Beckett left it out.

For the inside view on Beckett who better to turn to than those whose job it is to bring the work to life on stage? Numerous actors have delivered extraordinary Beckett performances, some of whom were even close friends of the writer, like Billie Whitelaw, Patrick Magee and Jack MacGowran.

New critical investigations and scholarly attempts to explain Beckett appear every other day, but on the whole I would prefer the intriguing, insightful account of Beckett given by his muse in her autobiography *Billie Whitelaw...Who He?*

Stephen Brennan, Johnny Murphy and Barry McGovern in Waiting for Godot, *1991*

There have been countless seminal Beckett productions but the Gate Theatre's 1991 production of *Waiting for Godot*, directed by Walter Asmus, seems unchallengable.

Waiting-ness. Has it something to do with Irish-ness? Or more to do with a congenital fear of missing the bus, brought on by too many hours spent in waiting on a 'banana' bus service (so called because they always travelled in bunches). Most unreasonably, C.I.E. became known as the 'Can It Endure' and 'Cycling is Easier'

Bus Company. I suspect Con Leventhal not only rang the bell but stopped the metaphorical bus when he emphasised the Irish-ness of the Godot tramps and referred to 'the Dublin lilt of the dialogue as translated by the author' and the appearance of 'Patrick Magee and Jack MacGowran in the author's own production!' In the fast-track culture of today's Ireland we must, we are told, 'hit the ground running'. McGovern, Murphy, Brennan and Stanford know what they're at, and in performing *Waiting for Godot* demonstrate to a supreme degree how, from the get go, to hit the stage waiting. It is always a good idea to bring a guide or guides when going walkabout, or, even, waitaround, and who better for the purposes of *Godot Go Deo* than Vladimir and Estragon in the shape of Barry McGovern and Johnny Murphy? This universally acclaimed, iconic duo have got to the heart of their fellow Dubliner's play with an intensity, commitment and understanding that borders on the awesome.

Cearbhall Ó Dálaigh has been attributed with the suggestion – made as evidence of an Irish influence in Beckett's work – that the name 'Godot' was wordplay on the Gaelic *go deo* meaning 'for ever'. Essentially *Godot Go Deo* is a book of illustrations based on the Dublin of Beckett's early life. Given that his later development as a writer was toward brevity and the barest of descriptive detail, I have concentrated on his pre-war publications as well as the haunts of his childhood and youth. The comic novel *Murphy* as well as *More Pricks Than Kicks* and its long unpublished predecessor *Dream of Fair to middling Women* provide the clearest guide to the topographical aspects of his city.

What ultimately drew me to Beckett's door, or more correctly inspired me to draw Beckett's doors – as well as the rest of his buildings! – was and is his combination of humour and honesty. There are no winners in the Beckett canon. Success is not an option, is it Samuel? And so, we go on failing, if only to try and fail better next time.

16

'...in winter, under my greatcoat, I wrapped myself in swathes of newspaper...The Times Literary Supplement was admirably adapted to this purpose.'

MOLLOY

COOLDRINAGH

Cooldrinagh is a salubrious place at which to begin. Samuel Beckett was born there on what he described as a bad Good Friday, 13th April 1906. Located outside Dublin in the tree-lined suburb of Foxrock, the Tudor House was built by his father, William Frank Beckett (1871–1933) in 1901 as a family home for his wife, May Roe Beckett (1871–1950) and their two sons Francis Edward (1902–1954) and Samuel Barclay (1906–1989). Large by Dublin standards, it served as a striking display of William's success as a quantity surveyor. If one is willing to press on, Cooldrinagh will bring any interested visitor lickety-split to the eye-filling landmark of Leopardstown Racecourse, which it overlooks.

THE DUBLIN MOUNTAINS

Bill Beckett brought his sons on regular peregrinations around the Dublin Mountains. These father and son outings were of importance to Sam not just for the magnificent country views, which became a recurring feature of his earlier writing, or for the air quality, colour and detail of the great mountain range. What mattered most was following in the boot steps of his father. Unlike May Beckett, who was severe and faced Samuel with an ongoing series of emotional stand-offs, Bill was easygoing and uncomplicated. 'If there is a paradise', wrote Beckett, 'father is still striding along in his old clothes with his dog. At night, when I can't sleep, I do the old walks again and stand beside him'.

20

FOXROCK STATION

From the age of five Sam attended a Foxrock kindergarten run by the Elsners, two German sisters who would later re-emerge in *Molloy*. Five years later, with his brother Frank, he attended Earlsfort House, a preparatory school near Harcourt Street station. At that time a rail line ran directly through Foxrock to terminate at Harcourt Street.

HARCOURT STREET STATION

Equally important in Beckett's Dublin was the Harcourt Street end of the 'Slow and Easy' line. It was only a minute's walk away from Earlsfort House, the school founded by a self-styled professor of French, Alfred Le Peton, who instilled in Samuel both a love of culture and an instinct for the avoidance of corporal punishment.

THE 'SLOW AND EASY'

Known colloquially as 'The Slow and Easy' the Dublin and South Eastern Railway was to emerge repeatedly in Beckett's writings. Throughout the various stages of his education, as schoolboy, undergraduate and lecturer, it took him back and forth to Dublin city.

The 'pretty little wayside station' of the radio play *All That Fall*, though dutifully renamed as 'Boghill' was, in fact, Foxrock. That station's waiting room also provided the setting for a scene in *Watt*. The Leopardstown racecourse could be seen from the elevated platforms at the Foxrock station. In *Watt* it could be spotted 'with its beautiful white railing, in the fleeing lights'.

One man's terminus is another man's starting point. Equally important in Beckett's Dublin is the Harcourt Street station, the end of the 'Slow and Easy' line, and the writer's emotional attachment to the station, and disappointment at its closure, was poignantly expressed in *That Time* '...all closed down and boarded up Doric terminus of the Great Southern and Eastern all closed down and the colonnade crumbling away so what next'.

TRINITY COLLEGE DUBLIN

Sent to the English-styled Portora Royal School in Enniskillen at the age of fourteen, Sam, like Frank, excelled himself on the rugby and cricket teams, but remained academically average and aloof from the school community.

On completing his secondary education, he may have followed the traditional Portoran route in 1923 by entering Trinity College Dublin, but soon showed he was not afraid to go down unused roads. In his third year the star cricket bowler transformed into something entirely different, a prize student.

In the course of his final year, his Professor of French, Thomas Rudmose-Brown, nominated Beckett for appointment as an exchange lecturer. He was to come first in his class and appointed in 1927 as *lecteur d'anglais* at the *Ecole Normale Supérieure*. Beckett was a frequent visitor to the home of his mentor on the Dublin Road in Malahide, and later referred to the area in the short-story "Fingal" in some detail.

JAMES JOYCE

Beckett spent almost two years in Paris where he met the poet, art critic and essayist, Thomas MacGreevy, from Kerry, who would become Beckett's closest confidante and introduce him to Jack B. Yeats and James Joyce.

Within a month of his arrival in Paris, Beckett had been accepted into Joyce's inner circle. He was commissioned to write a critical article on Joyce's *Work In Progress* which appeared as "Dante...Bruno. Vico..Joyce" in the Paris literary magazine *transition* in June 1929. Beckett's first short-story "Assumption" appeared in the same issue.

When Joyce decided on a musical evening, Beckett played piano while Giorgio sang Schubert.

Compelled by the terms of his award, Beckett returned to Dublin in 1930, as an assistant lecturer in French literature. On his return, he met Jack B. Yeats. Beckett identified with the darkness in Yeats's painting and understood it as the obverse side of life's coin, to which Beckett was also drawn albeit with a greater concentration, in his own development as a writer. Although Yeats did not reciprocate when it came to Beckett's work, they became good friends.

Beckett discovered the academic life was not what he had expected. He disliked the ordeal of lecturing and found his students problematic. Disenchanted, his thoughts turned to becoming a full-time writer.

BURKE

Although his athleticism would suggest otherwise, Beckett suffered minor, but constant, health problems in his twenties and thirties. He had boils, cysts, episodes of eczema and psoriasis – many of which afflictions would enter the catalogue of complaints by which Beckett charts the physical and mental decay of his characters. By the end of 1930, Beckett was unhappy with his chosen profession, lack of creative work, and far from tranquil relationship with his mother.

DREAM OF FAIR TO MIDDLING WOMEN

In January 1932 Beckett resigned from his teaching post at Trinity College. He decided to enter his full time profession as a writer in a city celebrated for its unswerving commitment to the arts. He therefore left one such fabled city of writers for another, moved to Paris and spent five months completing his first novel *Dream of Fair to middling Women* which remained unpublished until after his death.

In *Dream of Fair to middling Women* Beckett described one of the 'royal and fragile' figures of the title as a 'tuppenny fare' and the tram on which she travelled as a 'Cezanne monster'. Later in "A Wet Night", having been given a 'sign' by Bovril – as in the Bovril sign – Belacqua travelled down Pearse Street where, pestered by the pesky trams, he decided that when it came to public transport, he was with the buses.

'It's not easy being seen' may be another way of putting the 'agony of perceived-ness' theme explored by Beckett in *FILM* and elsewhere. Neither is it easy being green, or so the Polar bear in *Dream of Fair to middling Women* has it when, in a close encounter with a runaway tram, he takes exception to the conductor's parting shot of 'Next stop the Green.' One green however is as undesirable as another. 'If it's not the Steven's [sic] Green...'

'...it's Green's [sic] bloody library'. Exasperated, he decides that what the country needs is a change of the red variety.

The Polar Bear would not have appreciated the summation of a certain Dublin gastrologist who saw a seriously constipated young person in his surgery. The patient, a snooker diehard, was in considerable discomfort. Having decided the problem was one of diet, he inquired as to the sick man's daily intake. On his reply that he lived on snooker balls alone, the canny young medic asked which ones.

'Reds' he said vaguely 'Yellows, Blacks and Whites'.

'There's your problem' said the incisive professional, 'You're not getting enough Greens'.

In the summer of 1932 Beckett was forced to leave Paris. He did not have a *carte de séjour* and was faced with the prospect of returning to Dublin. His plan was to land a London publisher for *Dream of Fair to middling Women* en route to Cooldrinagh. This did not happen and by the end of August he was back being pestered by his mother May. Besieged by boredom, the pangs of loneliness and writer's block, he had to contend with a persistent cyst which required hospitalisation. He was dispirited and drinking heavily.

The family firm of Beckett and Medcalf, quantity surveyors, was located at number 6 Clare Street. Rather than Cooldrinagh, Beckett lived in garret lodgings on the top floor above his father's offices, while attempting to salvage and reshape *Dream of Fair to middling Women*. He occupied a large front room overlooking Greene's bookshop.

Despite its rejection by several London publishers, Beckett managed to successfully rewrite the book in parts for inclusion in his first collection of short stories *More Pricks Than Kicks* which was published by Chatto & Windus in 1934.

MORE PRICKS THAN KICKS

More Pricks Than Kicks, a collection of ten linked short stories serves as a relatively light and compelling appetiser for the weightier, more elliptical treats to come. The hero, Belacqua Shuah, is a melancholic Dublin intellectual who single-handedly charts the background – by taking us through a series of episodes in his life – to the dark heart of the entire Beckett universe. But don't expect a happy, shiny tour-guide.

Beckett's humour is often parodic and "Draff" is set in a nursing home but contains the image of a whispering priest in the Library of Trinity College. 'The ban' on Roman Catholics entering Trinity College under pain of excommunication applied during Beckett's time there.

In "Dante and the Lobster" it becomes the turn of Trinity's Senior Fellows - for whom 'buttered toast was good enough' - to take it on the chin but not, hopefully, in the mouth given that they had 'nothing but false teeth in their heads'.

Thomas Moore's statue appears several times in *More Pricks Than Kicks* as does Pearse Street. The adjoining urinal was first aid to many caught-short imbibers – and not lost on Joyce, being strategically placed 'under Tommy Moore's roguish finger' – and is referred to in "Ding Dong" as 'the underground convenience in the maw of College Street'.

In "A Wet Night" having disgorged himself from the 'hot bowels' of a pub, Belacqua checked to see if Moore's 'bull neck' fitted his head and shoulders. Through the years many Dubliners at Moore's plinth have also taken pause, and on rumination found like Belacqua that 'for the moment there were no grounds for his favouring one direction rather than another'.

Beckett visited art galleries avidly throughout his life. In *More Pricks Than Kicks* he uses his knowledge of artists and works of art in the collection of the National Gallery of Ireland to enhance his powers of description. The face of the pedlar woman in "Ding Dong" selling 'seats in heaven' reminds Belacqua of the Master of Tired Eyes's *Portrait of an Old Lady*. Botticelli, Uccello and other Italian school luminaries are redeployed by Beckett to help overcome the limitations of the printed word.

At Kennedy's 'lowly public' house in "A Wet Night" Belacqua lowers his porter, devours his paper, and reviews the latest innovations in corset building. Even in the early 1930s the crippling disadvantages of the pillar-of-flesh look were known to women, and the odd man.

Pie-eyed and legless on leaving Kennedy's, Belacqua went gently, if unsteadily, into that dark night. As he walked, childhood terrors returned to flood his soul, and the bottle in his pocket took on all the properties of a saving ordinance as he passed the Dental Hospital.

Despite the cold and damp of "A Wet Night" Belacqua stopped on the Baggot Street Bridge. Ignoring all citified intrusions he positioned his feet to dangle over the canal, and surveyed Leeson Street Bridge.

Belacqua felt a need for something special and remembered the bottle in his pocket while gazing at the Leeson Street Bridge, on a beautiful part of the canal, a sanctuary of calm and monument to beauty, worthy of Giovanni Antonio Canaletto.

LONDON

A lot happened in Beckett's life while work on *More Pricks Than Kicks* was in progress. From 1932, on the Beckett family were not singing from the same hymnal as Samuel.

The death of Bill Beckett in late June of 1933 devastated him. May's mourning was unrelenting and in time Beckett's psychosomatic illnesses returned. In order to enter psychoanalysis he moved to London, and, with money left by his father, lived for three years off the King's Road while attending Dr. Wilfred Bion of the Tavistock Clinic. In 1935 Jung gave a series of lectures at the Tavistock, which Beckett attended, including one, on the subject of the analysis of dreams, which was to directly influence the structure of Beckett's second novel *Murphy*. Beckett was aware of the high regard in which psychoanalysis was held at that time by artists and writers.

67

MURPHY

The garret in number 6 Clare Street, where Beckett had sat in splendid isolation above his family's offices and the rest of the world, is reminiscent of the garret described in *Murphy* as 'not an attic, nor yet a mansard, but a genuine garret'.

By the time *More Pricks Than Kicks* got into print, Beckett had already launched himself into the writing of *Murphy*, setting much of the action in the parts of London he had recently come to know. Discontinuing psychoanalysis before Christmas of 1935, he returned to Dublin in 1936 and completed *Murphy*, the hero of which, an Irishman in London, forsakes his girlfriend for the contemplative life as a male psychiatric nurse.

Murphy had been rejected by a long list of publishing houses including even 'Shatton & Windup' aka Chatto & Windus, before it was eventually published by Routledge in 1938.

Wynn's Hotel was where Neary, Wylie and Miss Counihan planned their London mission to restore Miss Counihan to Murphy.

You don't kick a man when he's down but neither should you dash your head against his buttocks. Oliver Sheppard's structure *The Fall of Cuchulainn* suffered just such an indignity when, in the General Post Office, Neary was compelled to body-check the Celtic superhero by the thighs and 'dash his head against his buttocks, such as they are'.

The Cuchulainn statue was created in the rebuilt GPO as a tribute to the executed signatories of the 1916 Easter rising. Beckett was disaffected with Irish nationalism and may have intended this episode to alert the reader to what he saw as the self-deceptions of nationalist mythology.

The Gate theatre receives only one mention from Beckett, in *Murphy*, despite its subsequent role as the good man's foremost champion: 'Didn't I have the dishonour once? Can it have been at the Gate?' Beckett was peripherally involved in a Gate production of *Youth's the Season* by Mary Manning Howe, for which he created the character, Egosmith.

PARIS

Beckett followed the same trajectory as Murphy at this time, moving between Ireland and England. He completed a six-month tour of German galleries in 1936 and on his return in 1937 to Dublin, decided to settle in Paris in the autumn of that year. In January 1938 Beckett was attacked on the avenue d'Orleans. He had been accosted by a pimp who stabbed him in the chest. While recuperating in hospital he corrected the proofs of *Murphy* and was visited by Suzanne Deschevaux-Dumesnil.

Within a year he and Suzanne took an apartment on the Rue des Favorites which was to be his home until 1961. 'I came back to Paris' he later commented and 'decided to settle down and make my life here'. He managed, despite the 'theocracy, censorship of books' and other equally unbearable aspects of Irish life, to return occasionally, but any doubts he may have entertained about the wisdom of leaving Dublin had vanished forever.

In the course of Beckett's public life, small talk about weather hasn't counted for much. As a result, this mid-1960s anecdote is of particular interest and may be as close as Sam ever got to singing a happy song. In London to attend a test match between England and Australia, Sam was walking with friends through Regent's Park en route to the Lord's cricket ground. The weather was reason enough to walk and talk as it was a beautiful summer's morning and everyone was in sparkling form. Beckett was moved to openly take pleasure in the company, blue skies and green tree-tops, those living monuments to the lofty ideals behind an ecosystem at the centre of a concrete jungle. Perhaps he gave a little whistle, to extol the beauty of the birdsong, or paused for dramatic effect before calling for a group-hug. Perhaps not. What we do know is that someone got carried away...

SOMEONE: Yes, on a day like today it feels good to be alive.
BECKETT: Well, I wouldn't go as far as that!

While living in France with Suzanne, writing in French as well as English, eating and drinking in the Left Bank cafes of which he was a *habitué*, Samuel Beckett by all accounts held out the hand of fellowship to those who crossed his path but ultimately kept himself to himself. He never ceased to write.

82

Bibliography

Bair, Deirdre, *Samuel Beckett: A Biography*. London: Jonathan Cape 1978

Brater, Enoch, *The Essential Samuel Beckett*. London: Thames & Hudson 1989

Dukes, Gerry, *Samuel Beckett*. London: Penguin 2001

Haynes & Knowlson, *Images of Beckett*. Cambridge: C.U.P. 2003

Kalb, Jonathan, *Beckett In Performance*. Cambridge: C.U.P. 1989

Knowlson, James, *Damned to Fame: The Life of Samuel Beckett*. New York: Simon & Schuster 1996

O'Brien, Eoin, *The Beckett Country: Samuel Beckett's Ireland*. Dublin: Black Cat Press; London: Faber & Faber 1986

Acknowledgements

Grateful thanks, first of all, to Paul Harris the Fingal County Librarian who, not for the first time, gave great help and guidance while I was preparing this book. *Godot Go Deo* has developed beyond all recognition thanks to the creative contributions of four people: the Dublin actor and leading interpreter of Beckett's work, Barry McGovern, was especially generous with his time; Jack Kirwan, the master skyscape painter (and spirit-invigorator) gave moral and practical help at a moment's notice; the expert photographer John Hackett shot my paintings with his characteristic efficiency and speed; and, yet again, Susan Waine, surely the most sought after design-artist around, still found time, and patience, to share a mad last-minute work-programme. I thank them all.

I used to chat about the 'difficult' Mr. Beckett with several people and *Godot Go Deo* is the fruit of many such conversations with: the Cork cartoonist Sean McArdle; John Healy; Gerard Dockery; Peter Somers; Sean Smyth; Gerard Maher; Michael Carrack and James Rickard. I should also thank: Johnny Murphy, Barry's wonderfully gifted opposite number and the other half of a perfect Beckett pair, who together proved as indispensable to Godot Go Deo as they already are to, arguably, the greatest play of the last century; Assumpta Hickey and Marian Caulfield of Fingal Libraries for their ongoing counsel and help; the Coolock Library gang; the late Samuel Beckett who I never met, though talking to Barry McGovern, who did, is the next best thing. My biggest debt, as ever, is to my family, Anne, Aisling and Cormac Lennon.

To dear Aisling